# CREATE A LIFE
## *You Can't wait to Live*

┅ ✦ ┅

## Ignite Your Passion, Peak Performance and Purpose.

# ZIG ZIGLAR

# Table of Contents

# Introduction

You are about to experience the life you can't wait to live—one filled with passion, peak performance and purpose.

After twenty-plus books on motivational subjects, and countless speeches and seminars on living the abundant and fruitful life, I've got some things to share with you that I believe will motivate you the same way they have motivated me.

Creating a life you can't wait to live is experienced by living with genuine passion, striving for peak performance, and fulfilling one's purpose.

I don't care what the field of endeavor is—sports, business, science, medicine, education, ministry, public service—I don't believe that anyone will perform at his or her peak without passion. Life's too tough to get to the top without passion. You're going to fail, be taken advantage of, be disappointed by people you trust, disappoint yourself, run out of resources—almost every day you're going to encounter a good, solid, logical reason why you ought to give up. And without passion, you just might. That's why passion is the prerequisite for peak performance.

Peak performance is dependent on passion, grit, determination, and a willingness to do something poorly until you can do it well. True peak performance is influenced by the condition of your physical, spiritual, business and family life.

The third part of the equation—purpose—is something I have come to believe is a key to the whole dynamic of motivation.

I've met people all through my life who had passion of a sort. But because their passion wasn't fueled by purpose, it would come and go in bits and pieces. They were trying to generate their passion out of their own energy day after day, something that's ultimately unsustainable. Scientists have yet to invent the world's first perpetual-motion machine—everything runs down or runs out of gas eventually, including human beings trying to maximize their peak performance day after day.

I believe this book can help motivate you to connect the dots in life, little by little. The end result will be a picture of beauty, purpose and fulfillment—a life you can't wait to live.

Zig Ziglar

# PASSION

*"Experience shows that success is due less to ability than to zeal. The winner is he who gives himself to his work, body and soul."*

CHARLES BUXTON

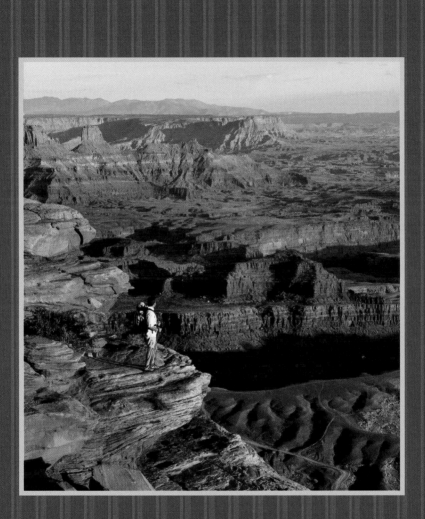

# Inspire Your Passion

"The core problem is not that we are too
passionate about bad things, but that we are
not passionate enough about good things."

LARRY CRABB

*Passion is underrated and under-rewarded.*
When a student with an average IQ performs magnificent feats in the academic world, give passion the credit. When you see an athlete with only average ability accomplish herculean tasks, give passion the credit. When you see a parent provide for his or her children despite physical or educational handicaps and road-blocks—obstacles that would stop an ordinary person in his or her tracks—give passion the credit.

I believe passion plays a significant part in all great accomplishments. Finding and developing passion is a journey, not an event. There is a process you must follow; some find it early, while some discover it much later. A noble passion, when found and developed, produces great joy and personal rewards and offers huge benefits to society as well.

I believe inspiration is the fuel of passion. If you think of passion as the flame that burns white hot in the heart of every person, inspiration is the fuel that keeps that flame alive.

Who is responsible for feeding inspiration to the flame of passion? You are! And if you don't, trust me—passion will, over time, become a distant and only occasional visitor to the house of your heart.

The question is, what are you doing to continually rekindle the passion of your life? What kind of inspiration are you providing for yourself that will keep you pursuing your dream? And if that passion dies, who's to blame?

*Here are four practical ways to inspire yourself—to feed the fires of passion burning within:*

## ⤙ 1: INVEST IN INSPIRATION

When people consider where to give some of their income for charitable or nonprofit purposes, they often think this way: "Gee, I don't feel very passionate about any of those causes, and I want to really feel strongly about what they're doing if I'm going to give my money to them." Have you ever heard that? Have you ever said that yourself?

If you treasure your money, you probably won't be giving much of it away. But if your heart gets involved as a result of coming to know the people you've been asked to help, you're much more likely to support them financially as well as physically and emotionally.

Do you see the difference? One view says, "When my heart kicks into gear (i.e., when I feel passionate), I'll invest my resources." But the correct view is, "I'm going to get involved because familiarity will increase my awareness, and once relationships are established I'll want to invest more than just my time and energy."

Let's say your passion is to own your own flower shop someday. Right now, you're not involved with flowers except as a hobby and impressing your neighbors with your gorgeous gardens every spring. But the children have left the nest and you know the time is right to make this move—to give wings to your passion. If I were to come to your house and spend an hour talking with you about your passion, I'd be looking for signs that you're investing your time, talent, and treasure. I'd be looking for bookshelves full of books on flowers and running a small business, magazine subscriptions on the same subjects, your class schedule for the course on entrepreneurship and small-business management that you're taking at the local community college, check stubs from your payment of dues to the appropriate floral associations, your applications to several local flower shops where you plan to work as an apprentice for the next year or so in order to get experience, the syllabus from a success and motivation seminar you recently attended…and on and on.

The fastest way I know to build and develop your passion in a given area of life is to invest your time, talent, and treasure in it.

## 2: INQUIRE FOR INSPIRATION

Do you want to keep your passion alive? Find a mentor—someone who has the same passion—and make some kind of arrangement to meet with that person on a regular basis for inspiration. There is nothing more inspiring to me than meeting with someone who is already successful at what I have a passion to do. Inspiration is caught better than it is taught.

There is no better way to stay inspired than by spending time in the presence of inspirational people. There is a healthy sort of peer pressure that keeps pushing us forward, a symbiotic effect that causes us to become more in the group (even a group of two—you and your mentor) than we could ever become by ourselves.

How do you find a mentor—someone to inspire you and help keep your passion aflame? In short, you ask. Obviously, you have to first find someone who is doing what you want to do, and preferably someone who does it well, shares your values, and has plenty of experience. Then, you ask. There are other resources available on mentoring relationships that you can read. But it boils down to your courteously inquiring as to whether this person would agree to spend a set amount of time with you on a regular basis to impart what he or she has learned about "the business"—whatever it is you have a passion to pursue. You'll be surprised how many people—especially retirees—would love nothing better than to have an outlet for imparting the passion they've been pursuing for decades.

Find someone inspiring and attach yourself to them, but only if you follow the Golden Rule of Apprentice-Mentor Relationships: don't become an apprentice unless you're willing one day to be a mentor yourself. That's what happens naturally in extended families. Apprentices grow up to become mentors—and it's the way passions stay alive for generations.

## 3: GET INVOLVED TO FIND INSPIRATION

Sometimes we have to get up and get involved in order to find inspiration and keep passion alive. The bigger the movement is in which we choose to get involved, the more we are inspired. Which inspires you more—being the only person sitting in a football stadium or being one of 70,000 screaming fans who are just as excited as you are about the home team?

Whatever your passion, get involved in it at a level that's bigger than you are. When you become part of something bigger than you are, you become accountable. You become inspired to do your best. You become motivated to not let others down. And that fuels your passion in ways that can't be described—it can only be experienced.

## 4: IMAGINE FOR INSPIRATION

One of the things that spurred me on as a rookie speaker was my imagination. I pictured myself speaking before crowds of thousands of people, knocking them dead with my humor and wisdom and humbly receiving their standing ovations. That didn't happen overnight, but I never allowed that picture to be erased from my mind. And eventually, everything I had imagined, and then some, became reality.

Bruce Barton made an interesting observation: "I do not like the phrase, 'Never cross a bridge until you come to it.' It is used by too many men as a cloak for mental laziness. The world is owned by men who cross bridges in their imaginations miles and miles in advance of the procession. Some men are born with more of an imagination than others, but it can, by hard work, be cultivated—not by mere daydreaming, not by lazy wondering, but by hard study and earnest thought."

Whatever your passion is, turn your imagination loose and let it inspire you to keep working to make your dreams become reality. *Remember: it's your job to fuel your passion, and inspiration is the fuel you need.*

"With the fearful strain
that is on me night and day,
if I did not laugh, I should die."

ABRAHAM LINCOLN

# Stress-
# the Enemy of Passion

"Blessed is the man who is too busy to worry
in the daytime and too sleepy at night."

EARL RINEY

*The enemies of passion will steal every good thing you possess if given the opportunity.* Your money, your reputation, your integrity, and your family are all at risk. Not only can they steal your passion, they are also capable of stealing your joy, your dreams, and your purpose for living. The thief I see robbing more people of their passion than anything else is stress—stress in all its forms.

I read a lengthy article in *Reader's Digest* once that documented that 90 percent of all doctor's visits can be attributed, directly or indirectly, to stress. Stress suppresses the body's immune system, interrupts your sleep, and makes you vulnerable to all manner of illnesses. You get sick and experience a whole host of other problems related to missing work and the inability to fulfill other responsibilities—and that just leads to more stress. It's a downward cycle that rarely has a happy ending.

To be fair, let's say the actual number was only 50 percent instead of 90 percent of illness related to stress. Can you imagine the impact on this nation if half of all doctor's visits were cancelled as a result of people learning to eliminate stress from their lives?

Productivity would skyrocket, money would be saved, people would be happier—the impact would reverberate throughout society like ripples on the surface of a pond.

I'm not suggesting that all stress is bad. Stress in the form of adrenaline can cause us to flee burning buildings and jump out of the way of oncoming traffic. It can also cause us to work hard to complete a project before a looming deadline. Some stress can be good. But when it is too frequent and meets with no resistance from us, it can destroy us by stealing our passion.

The message of Life 101 is that life is stressful, but stress can be managed so it doesn't rob us of our passion. I'm going to give you six ways to defend yourself against the attacks of stress.

# ➔ 1: WAIT TO WORRY

Most people spend so much time worrying that it never dawns on them that their worry could be producing stress and stealing their passion. They think worry is as normal as breathing—something you do if you're alive. I've heard my friend and mentor Fred Smith talk about worry many times.  Here's what he had to say:

"I ended up writing three little words on the inside of my skull. If you ever perform a craniotomy on me, you'll find them right there: WAIT TO WORRY. I found out I was doing my worrying before I had all the facts; I was free to wait to worry. As soon as I had the facts I had all the information I needed to work out a plan. When you have a plan, you don't have anything to worry about, so I'd stop worrying. I learned to wait to worry."

Fred is right—waiting is a lot less stressful than worrying. The next time you are attacked by stress, identify the source. Many times you will discover you are worrying about something that doesn't need to be worried about at all. Once you get all the facts, you may be glad you waited.

# 2: STAY IN THE GAME

Bonnie St. John Deane was a participant in the Paralympics. She was a one-legged skier who was competing against another one-legged skier. The other skier went first, and in the final run she fell. Bonnie confidently told her associates that she knew she was going to win because she wasn't going to fall. But she did fall and the other skier won. Bonnie's friends tried to console her by saying, "She was just a faster skier than you are." To this Bonnie adamantly responded, "No, she is not a faster skier. She just got up faster than I did."

I've never heard of anybody going all the way through life and not getting knocked down. Some people never get up and some get up so slowly it takes years and a lifetime of anger and bitterness before they recover. Bonnie St. John Deane assessed her circumstances correctly when she said, "People fall down. Winners get up. Gold medal winners get up fastest." Bonnie won the silver medal, was a Rhodes scholar, and became an award-winning IBM sales representative. She has been featured in *People* magazine, the *New York Times*, and *Ebony* magazine. With an attitude like hers, it's not surprising that she was once identified on *NBC Nightly News* as one of the five most inspiring women in America.

Getting up and getting back into the game removes the possibility of stress from long-term failure. Failure is not falling down—failure is not getting back up. Falling down is something that happened in the past. Regardless of what has happened in the past, if you are moving ahead confidently in the present, you have no cause to be stressed.

## ◄❾ 3: INSIST ON INTEGRITY

You can make a conscious decision in your life to do everything with integrity. When you do that, you inoculate yourself against any stress arising from guilt or shame. I've heard it said by many people that the great thing about telling the truth (living with integrity) is that you never have to remember what you said. If you're the kind of person who tells one person this and another person that, you're setting yourself up for big-time stress. You'll need to hire an assistant just to help you remember what stories you've told to whom. When you speak the truth, you speak and forget about it.

It's amazing how much stress you avoid when you play it straight. Do things with integrity, know what is wrong, practice what is right, and make your decisions accordingly. Your conscience will remain crystal clear, you'll live without regrets, and, as a result, your passion will remain alive and well.

# ➍ 4: STAY OUT OF DEBT

In our race to keep up with the Joneses, we put ourselves under mountains of stress. We go into debt in order to keep up appearances and then worry because we can't pay what we owe.

People today say they can't afford to stay out of debt, as if it's a disease that has crept into their life without their permission. "I must have it now!" is the battle cry of those who refuse to delay self-gratification.

When I look at the financial burdens American families put themselves under—thousands of dollars each year for activities for their children, dues at clubs, huge car payments, living in gated communities—I'm shocked. But I'm not surprised, then, when I hear about the stress the same families are living with. The never-ending quest to look good and feel good creates stress that completely negates the attempt to create the perfect lifestyle. We become hypocrites, trying to look good on the outside while dying on the inside.

No one can live a passionate life when he is worried about bill collectors and bankruptcy. If you want to stay free of stress, stay out of debt. It may take you months, even years, to get there. But the freedom of being debt free will allow you to unleash your passion in a way you'd forgotten could exist.

## ➥ 5: FEAR NOT

I don't think most people are in touch with what they truly fear. I don't mean the fear of tornadoes or black cats or roller coasters. I mean the fears that lurk inside each of us that keep us from launching ourselves into the great adventure called life! We fear failure, of course—perhaps most of all. But we also fear losing the security of our own inhibitions. We fear losing control, and we fear the future. We fear living with the tension that exists between what we know and what we don't know—the security of the present versus the insecurity of the future. Some people just can't handle the unknown, so they remain bottled up, confined to the reality of the past instead of the potential of the future. Life is often like having one foot on the dock and the other foot on a boat that is leaving. We want to leave, but our desire for the safety of the homeland keeps us tentative and indecisive—and often lands us in the water!

You may remember the 2002 Winter Olympic Games when 16-year-old Sarah Hughes skated her way to a gold medal. She stepped on the ice not believing she had a chance of winning any medal. She skated with reckless abandon, unconcerned about the live audience, the television audience, or for that matter, the judges.

She just gave it all she had. That sheer abandon she exhibited expressed the total joy she was feeling at the time and she turned in a spectacular performance, winning the gold. You may also remember that Michelle Kwan skated after Sarah and was expected to win the gold. She was a true champion, beloved by skating fans the world over, and the recipient of many medals in her career. But after Sarah Hughes's flawless performance, Michelle went out determined not to make any mistakes. She fell, and she took the bronze. I've always felt that while Sarah was focused on what to do, Michelle was focused on what to avoid doing. And it made the difference. The fear of failing inhibits and restricts performance and can throw cold water all over human passion.

## 6: HAVE THE FIRST LAUGH

Next to love, laughter has been described as the second most powerful emotion we can express. It has been said that laughter is like internal jogging—it stimulates the respiratory system, oxygenates the body, relaxes tense muscles, and releases pleasure producing chemicals in the brain. You cannot laugh and be mad, laugh and be tense, laugh and be stressed. Laughter is low calorie, caffeine free, and has no salt, preservatives, or additives. It's 100 percent natural and one-size-fits-all.

The most important use of laughter I have ever discovered is the ability to laugh at ourselves. I stopped taking myself too seriously years ago, and it was the best decision I ever made. Don't get me wrong—I'm still serious about what I do. But not so serious that I can't be the first one to laugh when I mess up (which happens all too often—it's why I spend so much time laughing!). When you're the first person to laugh at yourself, you leave little room for others to laugh at you.

If you will wait to worry, get up when you fall, live with integrity, live debt free, face the future with faith instead of fear, and be the first to infect others with laughter—your life will be a Stress-Free Zone.

"*The only thing we have to fear—is fear itself.*"

FRANKLIN DELANO ROOSEVELT

# *Watch What You Think*

⊹ ✦ ⊹

"You are not what you think you are. What you think, you are."

UNKNOWN

*Did you know that what you think powerfully impacts who you are?* What you think about yourself, what you think about the world, what you think about others, what you think about your prospects in life—*everything* you think has an impact on the kind of person you will become.

For instance, conduct a little research of your own. For the next week, pay special attention to how people answer the question "How are you?" or "How ya doin'?" That question gets asked and answered millions of times each day—in fact, you probably answer it yourself more than once every day. Listen to the answers people give to describe how they're doing:

"Not bad."
"So-so, I guess."
"Pretty good."
"Fantastic!"

"Terrible!"

"So far, so good."

"Not bad under the circumstances."

I'm going to guess that for every strong, positive, optimistic answer you hear from people you'll hear eight or ten that range from neutral to pessimistic. If people really are doing as poorly as I hear them say they're doing, I'm not sure why they get out of bed!

For longer than I can remember, I've been answering the "How are you?" question with something like, "Why, I'm doing better than good!" I answer that way because I truly expect things to be and become "better than good." I have learned through the years that, for reasons I can't scientifically or even theologically explain, how I expect things to be greatly influences how they become.

Because "better than good" is such an optimistic approach to life, I guarantee that you will be remembered when you say that's how you're doing. And it will catch on! Nothing is as infectious as optimism and a positive outlook.

*Sometimes, all it takes is a word, a phrase, or a thought planted in someone's mind to change his or her whole life.* It truly pays to watch closely what and how you think. It is said that Frank Outlaw expressed the power of our thoughts this way:

Watch your thoughts; they become words.
Watch your words; they become actions.
Watch your actions; they become habits.
Watch your habits; they become character.
Watch your character; for it becomes your destiny!

"Change your thoughts and
you change your world."

NORMAN VINCENT PEALE

# Attitude is Altitude

✦

"A pessimist is someone who complains about
the noise when opportunity knocks."

OSCAR WILDE

*Attitude is to life what altitude is to hot air ballooning—a way to remain free from disturbances that have the potential to send us crashing to the ground below.* If you are among the people in this life who feel like they are prisoners to the prevailing winds of circumstance, I have news for you. By adjusting your attitude, you can rise above that which seems inevitable and choose your destination instead of being taken where the winds of change dictate.

## A MATTER OF PERSPECTIVE

It's a mistaken notion to believe that happy people are those who experience one success or victory after another while unhappy people experience just the opposite. Research shows that happy people and unhappy people tend to have very similar experiences in life. The difference is perspective: unhappy people spend more time thinking about life's unpleasant events; they become introspective and self-centered in their thinking, and thus in their living. Happy people, on the other hand, take life's events in stride. They have a positive world view that allows room for disappointments and failures along the way. They seek out and depend upon facts that bolster their perspective on life; they are outward focused and centered on others.

To put it another way, ***positive people don't react to life; they respond.*** Responding is positive; reacting is negative. Think of the word *reactionary*. What image does it bring to mind? It's someone with his heels dug in, someone in a defensive posture, someone who strikes back. But a responder is one who engages, one who takes the offense, someone who reaches out rather than striking back.

Optimists love facts because they are like the pieces of life's jigsaw puzzle—you need them all to put the puzzle together. Optimists will lay all the facts on the table, not for the purpose of saying, "Woe is me," but in order to start putting together the strategy for the next day, week, month, and year. When you get right down to it, optimists are happy people. At least, that's been my experience.

Optimists really believe the goal they are working toward is going to come to pass in one form or another. I will tell you that if you want to have passion in life, you can't be a pessimist. Pessimism will drain the passion out of you like oil out of a crankcase. Just try getting a life in gear that is missing the oil of passion and see how far you get. I can't emphasize enough the impact of attitude on the journey toward peak performance. Attitude is a mental outlook—a frame of mind. It's how you think based on what you know to be true.

In your life and mine, friend, attitude is altitude. It's all we need to stay above the fray going on beneath.

By this point in the book I hope I've whetted your passion's appetite for creating the life you want to live. Because now it's time to start letting passion do what it is supposed to do: be the fuel that propels us to peak performance!

"*The greatest discovery of my generation is that a human being can alter his life by altering his attitudes of mind.*"

WILLIAM JAMES

# PEAK
# PERFORMANCE

"*People were designed for accomplishment, engineered for success, and endowed with seeds of greatness.*"

ZIG ZIGLAR

# Develop a Passionate Plan

✦

"Plan ahead—it wasn't raining when Noah built the ark."

RICHARD CUSHING

*There's no sense in having passion in life if you don't apply it.* That's like filling up the tank of your car with the highest octane gas and then not going anywhere. The whole concept of true *peak performance* implies that there is something you want to do, somewhere you want to go with your life. And that suggests the need for knowing how to plan—and how to remain flexible enough to adjust your plan as the need arises.

I have met some people who are full of good intentions. There are a million things in life they want to do, but they just never get around to doing them. Some of that is due to laziness, but I believe the majority is due to fear—the fear of failure, the fear of not planning well enough to cover every contingency along the way, the fear that when they arrive the destination may look different than they hoped it would when they began. As a result, they postpone the journey all their lives because they can never plan thoroughly enough to remove all contingencies.

Joe Sabah has written, "You don't have to be great to start. But you do have to start to be great." Too many people want to wait until everything is perfect—all possible contingencies are removed—before beginning. Even in the most critical activities of life (for example, brain surgery and space flight), contingencies are part of the process. Doctors don't know with 100 percent accuracy what they'll find when they operate. And NASA engineers, as history has tragically shown us, aren't certain that everything will go as planned on space flights. But they don't let those unknowns keep them from starting.

There is one sure way in life I know of to never reach your peak performance, and that is never to start!

## DYNAMICS OF STRATEGIC PLANNING

I'm calling the following four points "dynamics" instead of "steps," because they are bigger than steps; they permeate the planning process from beginning to end. There is never a time in the execution of your plans—from dream to destination—that you will not experience all four of these dynamics:

### 1: HAVE FAITH

This boils down to having faith or confidence. But you are going to have to have it in the planning stages, the execution stage, the obstacle stage, the reversal stage, and in the give-up-the-ship stage.

### 2: TAKE ACTION

The moment you stop taking action, everything in your plan stops. Make sure something is happening all the time toward the accomplishment of your plan.

### 3: LEARN AS YOU GO

The bottom line here is to learn from your mistakes and failures. There has never been a perfect human plan and never will be. Edison's light bulb was a great start, but it continues to be refined today. Life is a classroom—only those who are willing to be lifelong learners will move to the head of the class.

# 4: PERSEVERE WITH HOPE

If you aren't willing to fight for your plan from start to finish, there is reason to wonder if it ever should have been launched.

It doesn't matter what your plan is—to lose weight, stop smoking, start a business or a ministry, go back to school—you will need to keep these four dynamics alive throughout the process. And if you do, you will succeed.

## ...YOU DO HAVE TO START TO BE GREAT.

"*Planning* is bringing the future into the present so you can do something about it now."

ALAN LAKEIN

# Goal Setters
# are Picture Painters

⊶ ✛ ⊷

"Setting a goal is not the main thing. It is deciding how you will go about achieving it and staying with that plan."

TOM LANDRY

*Florence Chadwick was no stranger to goal setting.* An American swimmer, she was the first woman in history to swim the twenty miles across the English Channel from France to England (in 1950) and then a year later swim the same distance from England to France. And in 1954 she attempted unsuccessfully to be the first person to swim across Lake Ontario. Between the English Channel successes and the Lake Ontario failure, Florence set yet another unbelievable goal: be the first woman to swim the twenty-one miles from Catalina Island to the west coast of California. On the morning of July 4, 1952, the ocean between Catalina and California was shrouded in fog—Florence could hardly see the boats accompanying her to keep away the sharks. Fatigue wasn't a big problem, but the bone-chilling temperature of the water was. After fifteen hours of nonstop swimming, she succumbed to the temperature of the water and asked to be pulled into one of the boats. Her mother and trainer, in a boat alongside her, urged her to keep on as they were getting near the coast. Yet all Florence could see was fog—she could have been twenty yards or twenty miles from the shore.

She was pulled out of the water too cold and tired to continue. Later, she realized that she was only half a mile from completing the swim and achieving her goal. When she learned how close she was when she quit, she blurted out, "I'm not excusing myself, but if I could have seen the shore, I might have made it!" It wasn't the distance or the cold that ultimately did her in—it was the fog. *When Florence Chadwick lost sight of her goal, she lost the will to continue.*

Here's the postscript: two months later, on a day when there was no fog in sight, she completed the swim, setting a new speed record for the Catalina-California crossing. Same island, same coast, same distance, same body of water. The only difference between victory and defeat was the ability to see her goal.

I share this story because it's like a prism—it reflects a number of different truths about setting goals. I'd like to share four of them with you:

## 1: FIND THE GOAL

There is no end to the kind and number of goals we can set in our lives. Florence Chadwick looked for things that hadn't been done in her area of expertise—first woman to swim the English Channel in both directions, first woman to swim Lake Ontario, first woman to swim from Catalina to California. Setting those goals forced her to continue to develop herself as a swimmer.

## ↔ 2: OVERCOME OBSTACLES TO THE GOAL

There are also any number of things that can derail our pursuit of a goal. We have to be informed and prepared in order to not be surprised when obstacles arise. It probably never crossed Florence Chadwick's mind that fog would keep her from reaching her goal.

## ↔ 3: KEEP YOUR EYE ON THE GOAL

Continual review and progress checks are critical. When we lose sight of the goal or it gets obscured by something unexpected, something happens emotionally. Keeping the goal in sight, literally and emotionally, serves to keep us energized.

## ↔ 4: SET AN ATTAINABLE GOAL

Fourth, goals can be ultimately achieved even if we fail the first time. There is a difference in swimming the Catalina-California crossing and swimming it on the first attempt. Failure to define the goal carefully can result in such discouragement, if we fail, that we won't try again. Fortunately, Florence Chadwick's goal was to swim the crossing, not swim the crossing on the first attempt—which allowed her to try again and succeed.

## THE POWER OF A PAINTING

Goal setters are picture painters. They are artists of life who use a canvas, brush, and paints to create images of what they want life to be like. But they don't paint literal pictures—they paint mental, spiritual, and emotional ones. They create images of how their lives will be different if they do thus and so, and it is those images that inspire them to set a goal and achieve it.

Goal setters often take the image they've created in their mind and reduce it to writing. They describe, in their own words, how life will be once their goal is reached. This verbal picture becomes a tool in their hand to review, amend, and expand while they are working toward their goal.

The power of a literal picture made the difference in my reaching a goal that had eluded me for many years. I had weighed well over 200 pounds—way too much for my five-foot-ten inch frame—for far too long. I went on many different diets and periodically lost large amounts of weight, only to gain it back. Later I discovered that the problem had been with the picture I was painting in my mind.

The lesson? The same as with my losing weight experience: don't picture the negative, the thing you *don't* want to do or be like. Instead, paint a picture in your mind of what you want to achieve—what your goal will look like in your life when you reach it.

Those episodes taught me something critical about setting and reaching goals: keep a picture of the goal in sight. Florence Chadwick quit her quest for the California coast a half mile too soon because she lost sight of her objective. And you may abandon your goal before you reach it if you don't paint a picture of it and keep it in sight.

Let me make a very strong point: *in the achieving of your goals, it's not what others believe you can do; it's what you believe you can do.*

*Pursue that goal, and every other goal imaginable will fall into place. You may never climb Mount Everest, but you will be a "peak" performer.*

"Aim at heaven and
you will get earth thrown in.

*Aim at earth and you will get neither."*

C. S. LEWIS

# Refuse to Give Up

◆

"The men who try to do something and fail are infinitely better than those who try nothing and succeed."

LLOYD JONES

*How many times have you witnessed a person who was a slow starter (translation: "failure") who later bloomed and became a raging success in his or her chosen field?* More times than you can count, if you're like me. And I've read about countless others.

Take New England Patriots quarterback Tom Brady, for instance. By the age of 28, he had led the Patriots to three Super Bowl titles and been the Most Valuable Player in two of them. He's been featured on *60 Minutes*, hosted *Saturday Night Live*, had an audience with the pope, has a sixty-million-dollar football contract, and was invited to the 2004 State of the Union Address. But such was not always the case for this modest QB. Though he was an All-American high school quarterback, he received no attention at all from college scouts. If his father hadn't put together a videotape of Tom and sent it off to sixty college coaches, he might never have played college football. He was ultimately signed to play at Michigan but not as the starter.

When it came time for the NFL draft, the scouting report on him read, "Poor build, very skinny and narrow, lacks mobility and the ability to avoid the rush, lacks a really strong arm." He sat through six rounds of the draft before he was picked as the 199th player chosen—and again, not as a starter. When the starter for the Patriots was knocked out with an injury, Brady finally got his chance—and the rest is history.

Here's how Tom Brady sums up his slow start to NFL stardom: "Don't let other people tell you what you're capable of. As long as you believe in yourself and work hard to achieve whatever you set your mind to, you just keep plugging away. It may not be up to your timetable, but you can get it done."

In fact, I believe there is a significant connection between passion, peak performance, and failure. Often, people with great passion for their calling will fail miserably at it before they achieve peak performance. Why? Because they often start too strong and fast. Maybe they lack the maturity that years of living will bring. Maybe they lack technical training or know-how. Maybe they lack experience. But they have so much passion that they rush out and trip all over themselves because they just don't know any better. Yes, they fail—but their passion keeps them in the game; they refuse to take no for an answer.

## THE VALUE OF FAILING

Failure is one of life's greatest teachers as long as we are not crushed by it—as long as we learn from it. I like to divide the world into two camps: learners and nonlearners. When the learners do something that is not wise, and failure is the result, they don't do it again. They learn the lesson. And when they do something that works, they take note and try to repeat it. In other words, they don't treat life like a tunnel—a tube that never gets narrower. They treat life like they're heading into a funnel. As they exclude choices and actions that don't work, they are continually narrowing the range of options: they're throwing out the stupid and keeping the stupendous. Eventually they hit their stride as peak performers because they don't do stuff that doesn't work. The real question in life is not whether you are a success or a failure but whether you are a learner or a nonlearner.

Speaker Steve Brown has said that anything worth doing is worth doing poorly—until you can learn to do it well. Since most people fear failure like the plague, Steve Brown's words are good ones: they actually give you permission to fail. If you accept the notion that failure is just a pit stop on the way to the winner's circle, then you are prepared to create the life you want to live.

You have it in you to achieve peak performance in the arena of your dream. But only if you do not let temporary failures quench your passion.

"I don't know the key to success,
but the key to failure is trying to
please everybody."

BILL COSBY

"Our business in life is not to get ahead of others,
but to get ahead of ourselves,
to break our own records,
to outstrip our yesterday and our today."

STEWART B. JOHNSON

# Cultivate Good Habits

"The strength of a man's virtue should not be measured
by his special exertions, but by his habitual acts."

BLAISE PASCAL

*I have never known a true peak performer who did not invest consistent energy into the cultivation of good habits.* Notice I didn't say "invest energy into getting rid of bad habits." Why? Because with the cultivation of every good habit (for example, getting plenty of rest at night) a bad habit disappears (sitting up watching late-night talk shows on television). It was the sixteenth century scholar Erasmus who said, "A nail is driven out by another nail; habit is overcome by habit."

*It is always in your best long-term interest to do your very best— to get in the habit of being a peak performer. And here's how:*

## 1: THE "DAY BEFORE VACATION" PLAN

Let's say you're planning on going on a week's vacation beginning next Monday, so Friday will be your last day at work. Typically, late Thursday afternoon or evening, you'll make a to-do list of everything that needs to get done on Friday before you leave for a week. It's the only way to come back from vacation and not have your fellow employees mad at you because you left so many loose ends and irons in the fire that they didn't know how to deal with. Friday turns out to be a peak performance kind of day because you're so looking forward to vacationing in peace.

Question: why don't we operate that way every day? The "Day Before Vacation Plan" should be our daily approach to accepting responsibility and earning our pay—leaving work with everything taken care of that was in your power to do.

## ✎ 2: THE "NO OTHER OPTION" PLAN

Perform on your job as if it were the only job available. If you work as if your job and your life depend on keeping that job (and doesn't it?), you'll strive to do your best daily.

## 3: THE "LIVE AND BREATHE THE JOB" PLAN

Do the little things that are not in your job description. Translation: take ownership! I played golf recently at a prestigious club where one of our foursome was the primary owner of the club. We all noticed throughout the game that anytime he saw even a small piece of trash he would pick it up. One of the other men made the comment, "You can always tell who the owner is."

When your employer sees you assuming ownership and responsibility for the company's image, reputation, products, and profitability, your value to the company will skyrocket.

## 4: THE "DON'T WORRY, BE HAPPY" PLAN

Get up on the right side of the bed every morning. Begin and end the day in a positive frame of mind. Greet your coworkers cheerfully in the morning and bid them good night in the evening. This is a habit that is easily cultivated.

# ↬ 5: THE "I AM WHO I AM" PLAN

Finally, live one life, not two. What you do in your private life, away from work, is just as important as what you do at work. In time, if you are living two lives, it will become evident. If I followed you around from the moment you left work until you returned the next morning—and did that for three months—I ought to see the same person in both places. Be true to yourself and those with whom you work.

*There are several other habits which are indispensable in creating the life you want to live:*

## THE HABIT OF STAYING MOTIVATED

I am often asked at seminars, "Can everybody be motivated?" The answer is "Yes!" When we find people who are hard to motivate, it means we have not found, or they are not in touch with, their "hot button"—that emotional switch that is wired to their deep-seated dreams, desires, or calling. If we can find that hot button and then show them ways to accomplish what is important to them, they will be motivated. Once people learn the emotional and practical benefits of staying motivated, they will begin to motivate themselves.

# THE HABIT OF LISTENING

During the Lee Iacocca years at the Chrysler car company, management went to the men and women on the assembly lines—the people who actually build the cars—and asked them for suggestions on how to produce a better car. And they got an earful about how the assembly lines were organized.

Back injuries (lost work time) were common among the assembly-line workers because they had to bend over to work on the cars as they came down the line. Other workers, who worked in pits beneath the assembly lines, complained of the dangers of slipping on constantly wet floors, resulting in falls (more lost work time). So management listened—and acted. In some places the assembly lines were raised to waist level so the cars could be worked on without having to bend over. And in other places the lines went over the workers' heads so they could work on the bottom of the cars, eliminating the dangerous pits.

As a result, absenteeism due to injury was cut dramatically and the expense of hospitalization and medical costs were cut by 90 percent. When employees were no longer falling and working with sore backs, morale increased. When morale increased, motivation surged and the quality of the cars coming off the line increased significantly. Quality went up, profits soared, and stockholders were ecstatic. As a result of listening to their employees, Chrysler started producing "better than good" cars.

Who would have thought there would be a connection between healing sore backs and ecstatic stockholders? And it happened because Chrysler took time to listen.

## THE HABIT OF LEARNING

George Eliot said, "It's never too late to become the person you could have been." And I have never seen that truth personified more clearly than in the life of Laurie Magers.

Laurie only finished the tenth grade. Twenty-eight years ago she came to work at our company as my secretary. In time, she became my administrative assistant, and today she is my "I-don't know-what-I'd-do-without-her" executive assistant. A few years ago, while doing an evaluation of all our company's key personnel—and that definitely includes Laurie—she was rated at a level of effectiveness that suggested she had earned a master's degree.

Over the years, Laurie has taken classes and attended courses that continue to qualify her for more and more responsibility. She has self-educated herself to be increasingly more qualified to handle tasks that might have required years of formal education. Frankly, I'm amazed at what she can do.

For instance, no proposal leaves our company until Laurie Magers signs off on it. She approves every aspect of the print portion—language, style, grammar, clarity, and readability. Then she confers with accounting and checks any legal loose ends. Anything in written form involving company policy crosses Laurie's desk before it leaves our building.

Now how did someone with a tenth-grade education become qualified to do all that? Through the habit of learning. Laurie Magers has made learning a "habitual" part of her lifestyle. She reads, studies, questions, attends, critiques, inquires—she educates herself beyond her present responsibilities in order to become overqualified and ripe for a promotion. And she has been rewarded for her efforts.

Ask Laurie. She'll tell you it is not where you start—it's where you want to go and your willingness to work to get there that will make a difference.

## THE HABIT OF READING

For the past thirty years I have read an average of three hours daily, seeking information that will inspire, instruct, and encourage me so I can then use that same information to inspire, instruct, and encourage others. If an average reader (average is about 220 words per minute) will read twenty minutes every day, he or she will read 22 hundred-page books each year. Can you imagine the edge that would give them when it comes to effectiveness in our knowledge-based society?

Consider this truism: the person who doesn't read is no better off than the person who can't read. We consider ourselves a literate nation, but is a literate nation of nonreaders really literate? Information is exploding so fast that anyone who does not read and keep up is rapidly falling behind.

# THE HABIT OF REDEEMING TIME

The average person in America today spends well over an hour a day in his or her automobile commuting to and from work. With CD players, cassette players and DVD players in our cars, now there is no end to ways to redeem the drive-time hours.

I call this enrolling in Automobile University. And besides the intellectual stimulation and advances in learning you'll experience, there's another benefit: research shows you are four times less likely to be involved in an auto accident that causes you bodily injury if you listen to informative or inspirational material than if you talk on a cell phone.

# THE HABITS OF HEALTH AND REST

There's compelling evidence for the connection between the physical, mental and spiritual parts of our lives. Health is holistic. You must seek to be healthy in all areas of your life if you are going to be a peak performer.

A lack of sleep results in poor decision making and impacts other areas of our lives. If we're tired we're more likely to be irritable, to put off exercise, and to overeat. But if we've developed a plan for getting plenty of rest, we'll rise in the morning excited and ready to face a new day.

## THE HABIT OF SELF-DISCIPLINE

You may or may not see your daily work as noble. But you should (as long as it is moral and legal!). You can turn the lowliest job into the most honorable vocation through your own self-discipline—the development of habits and practices that make you the best there has ever been at that job. Peak performance has nothing to do with the job and everything to do with the person who is performing it—and how they're performing.

"I believe long habits of virtue have a sensible effect on the countenance."

BENJAMIN FRANKLIN

"*Freedom is not the right to do what we want but what we ought.*"

ABRAHAM LINCOLN

# The Power of Grit

❧ ✦ ❧

"With true grit you persist until you catch a glimpse of your potential.
That is when passion is born."

FRED SMITH

*Grit is the bedrock of success; this should not surprise us.* Recent research suggests that a mere 25 percent of the differences between individuals in job performance can be attributed to IQ. Intelligence accounts for only a fraction of the reason for success. Grit has value for people at all levels of ability.

However, while it is true that study after study of high achievers in various fields shows that the one common characteristic of their success was that they were tenacious, these same studies suggest that determination motivates people to incredible feats of creativity. Take Barbara Corcoran, for example:

Barbara sold her New York City real estate company in 2001 for $70 million. Not bad, considering she began it with a $1,000 loan twenty-five years earlier. But she came close to losing it all following the stock market crash of 1987. She owed $300,000 and was writing a good-bye speech to her employees when she remembered something from her childhood. Her grandfather's neighbor had had a litter of four puppies to sell and invited a crowd of interested buyers to come at one time to look at them. Supply and demand took over. Since there were only four puppies and three times that many interested buyers, every one became the pick of the litter. Corcoran set her good-bye letter aside, added up the value of the eighty-eight different apartments her company had for sale in seven different buildings, divided the total by eighty-eight, and priced them all equally regardless of size or shape. She then ran an ad announcing the once-in-a-lifetime opportunity. Hundreds of people lined up to get one, and she netted over $1 million in one weekend. "I was able to open up two more offices in the depths of the recession. The worst hours became the best hours, simply because of persistence," she said.

Most great achievements in life do not occur "inside the box." When Jeff Bezos founded Amazon.com, he attracted hordes of buyers with creative innovations—and his creativity has continued unabated: one-click buying, free shipping, gift wrapping of purchases, customer reviews of products, ability to purchase a used book or CD cheaper than a new one, and on and on.

Get outside the box on your quest—only there will you likely find the creative ideas you need for the breakthrough you are seeking.

## TIME AND DETERMINATION

Peter Doskoch cites what experts call the "decade rule"—meaning that "it takes at least a decade of hard work or practice to become highly successful in most endeavors, from managing a hardware store to writing sitcoms—and the ability to persist in the face of obstacles is almost always an essential ingredient in major achievements."

The interesting phenomenon regarding the decade rule is this: looking ahead, ten years looks like forever. Looking back, it seems like the blink of an eye. Therefore, don't let the "long haul" dissuade you from reaching your goal. When you get there, you'll remember little of the blood, sweat, and tears you expended. You'll be basking in the rarified air of success as you stand on the performance peak toward which you've been traveling.

"Press on.
Nothing in the world can take the place
of persistence."

CALVIN COOLIDGE

# PURPOSE

*"Purpose is the place where your deep gladness meets the world's needs."*

FREDERICK BUECHNER

# Passion, Peak Performance and Purpose

+=— ⁘ —=+

"Get the pattern of your life from God,
then go about your work and be yourself."

PHILLIPS BROOKS

*Passion supplies energy and drive, and peak performance is the result of the application of passion.* But without purpose, peak performance becomes a hit-or-miss affair.

It's my contention that peak performance in life only comes when I'm exercising my passion toward that which I believe is my purpose in life. And, by that definition, I think many people in life have never tasted peak performance. Why? Because they have not searched for and discovered their purpose. And that may be because they never knew, or chose to believe, that they *have* a purpose in life!

Would you sink into deep despair tomorrow if you were told you can no longer work at your present job? Would you keep doing what you're doing at half the salary? Are you going to continue what you're doing because you have to (financially) or because you want to (you can't see yourself doing anything else)? Regardless of how well you do your current "thing," is there something you dream about doing that's completely different—something you hope to do when you retire and can "do what I really want to do"?

How you answer those questions has a lot to do with whether you're performing at your peak, because they have a lot to do with whether you think you're accomplishing a divine purpose for your life or not.

## THE POWER OF ONE

There is awesome power in every single person. If you don't think so, look at the difference one person has made throughout history:

- ✣ In 1645, one vote gave Oliver Cromwell control of England.
- ✣ In 1776, one vote gave America the English language instead of German.
- ✣ In 1845, one vote brought the state of Texas into the Union.
- ✣ In 1868, one vote saved President Andrew Johnson from impeachment.
- ✣ In 1875, one vote changed France from a monarchy to a republic.
- ✣ In 1941, one vote saved the Selective Service System just twelve weeks before Pearl Harbor was attacked.

- And, unfortunately, in 1923 one vote gave Adolph Hitler control of the Nazi Party in Germany.

Those are just a few instances in which one person has made a huge, inestimable difference for good or, in some cases, for bad in the affairs of this world. At the time the people casting those votes did so, they likely didn't realize the ramifications of what they were doing. Rarely do we have that kind of insight at the time we act.

You are not just "one"—you are a significant one with an important purpose to fulfill.

## PURPOSE AND PERMISSION

If you're ever approached by a young man named Kyle Maynard who asks you if you want to wrestle, my advice is, don't!—even though he has no arms below the elbows or legs below the knees. Kyle Maynard is a congenital amputee—a condition that affects one in every 2,000 births, but rarely in as extreme a case as Kyle's. He has only the upper part of both arms and the upper part of both legs, yet he became a championship wrestler in his Georgia high school. The title of his new book, *No Excuses* (September 2005), pretty much says it all. His parents raised him not to make excuses, and he's made none.

As a kid, Kyle was all about sports. He played goalie in street hockey games with his friends, and even played on a football team in the sixth grade. He also started wrestling in the sixth grade— and lost his first thirty-five matches. But by the time he got to high school, it was a different story. He and his father, a former wrestler, had worked out a weight-training program that made all the difference, and he and his coach worked out new moves and holds unique to his physical condition. In his senior year on the varsity wrestling team, he won thirty-five matches and lost sixteen. He qualified for the state championships and won his first three matches—but lost his final match (wrestling with a broken nose) in a thriller.

After describing Kyle Maynard to you, I hardly think anything more needs to be said about self-esteem. Unfortunately, however, there are lots of people with no physical challenges who don't view themselves as "normal" as this congenital amputee does. What does it take to see ourselves in a positive light—to have a positive self-esteem—in spite of the limitations and difficulties all of us experience? What does it take to believe that we are significant enough to have a purpose to fulfill?

"*Great is the art of beginning,
but greater is the art of ending.*"

HENRY WADSWORTH LONGFELLOW

# Discover Your Calling

✥

"If a man is called to be a street-sweeper, he should sweep streets
even as Michelangelo painted, or Beethoven played music,
or Shakespeare wrote poetry. He should sweep streets so
well that all the hosts of heaven and earth will pause to say,
here lived a great street-sweeper who did his job well."

MARTIN LUTHER KING, JR.

*We could count on one hand the number of people in history whose calling in life was handed to them on a silver platter— like a telegram arriving from heaven.* A somewhat larger number have had a "Eureka!" moment in which they somehow knew what they were called to do for the rest of their lives. But for most of us, discerning our calling in life is a process, something that becomes clear over time.

Opportunities are not synonymous with calling. There are more opportunities in life than any of us could possibly take advantage of. And many people never find their true calling in life because they don't measure opportunities against purpose. If you are doing things without a good reason (purpose), you won't have the emotional and spiritual energy (passion) to sustain the work. Nothing worthwhile in life was ever achieved without a compelling reason to achieve it.

Dr. Howard Hendricks, a well-known professor of theology and leadership coach, said this: your career is what you are paid for; your calling is what you are made for. The goal is to have your career and your calling overlap as close to 100 percent as possible so you get paid to do what you were made to do. Some rare individuals start at 100 percent overlap, but most begin somewhere below 50 percent and spend a few years closing the gap between career and calling.

For instance, if your heart's desire is to travel the world, there are lots of jobs that can help you achieve your dream. Working for an airline is possibly the most obvious. Being a storm trooper (an individual who works for insurance companies assessing the property damage done by hurricanes, tornados, fires, and other natural disasters) or even a missionary will take you places even you never considered.

Why be involved in anything in life that does not help you accomplish your life purpose? Therefore, a key question to ask is: what really matters to you? What "floats your boat," as they say? What do you do when you have free time? What do you dream about doing when you're stuck in a traffic jam? Whatever it is, that's where your heart is; that's what you're passionate about. And somewhere, connected to that passion, is your calling.

We need to become attuned to those moments in life that reveal our values and our passion. It's one thing to identify those moments and take note of what they are saying to us, but it's another to respond to them—to use those moments as a launching pad for action. Sometimes you may not like what you learn about yourself, and that's important too. The important thing is to have your radar on and be in touch with what your heart is telling you about who you are and what fulfills you—and what doesn't—on a daily basis.

Even if we are content in what we are doing, we should be continually looking for ways we can make an uplifting contribution to our world. We should be asking questions like: What is it that leaves my heart feeling full and my spirit at peace? How can I use my gifts and abilities in a productive and profitable way? How can I move beyond my current level of abilities to make an even greater contribution in the future? What new interests or challenges have come into my life lately to which I need to pay attention? Could they be doorways or pathways to a new and more fulfilling calling? Am I sensitive to things happening around me—those divine interventions that could be signposts or wake-up calls? To what degree am I already fulfilling the highest calling for my life of which I am currently aware?

Think about what makes your heart truly glad. Then think about the world's needs. To what degree is there convergence between the two? Man's greatest calling comes when he discovers and confirms that what he was put on this earth to do is meeting a genuine need of other people. We discover value and satisfaction in our calling when we can honestly say, "There is nothing I would rather do." The sense of "deep gladness" you get from fulfilling your calling both inspires and energizes you to continue onward, regardless of the personal cost.

Think back on the happiest moments in the tapestry of your life. In the thousands of moments that are woven together to make up your story, there are undoubtedly some where time seemed to stand still; where you felt like you were outside yourself, watching yourself doing something truly significant, truly gratifying, truly important. I believe those are the moments in which you find yourself standing at the crossroads of purpose, passion, and peak performance; where those three dynamics merge and become one.

"*Life is not just a few years to spend on self-indulgence and career advancement. It is a privilege, a responsibility, a stewardship to be lived according to a much higher calling, God's calling. This alone gives true meaning to life.*"

ELIZABETH DOLE

"*You will become as small as your controlling desire; as great as your dominant aspiration.*"

JAMES ALLEN

# The Power of People

+=— ❖ —=+

"You can make more friends in two months by becoming more interested in other people than you can in two years by trying to get people interested in you."

DALE CARNEGIE

*I have yet to see a commercial on television advocating the power of relationships as a way to fight winter colds and flu.* Yet there seems to be plenty of evidence to support the idea. A *New York Times* article, "Social Ties Reduce Risk of a Cold," reported: *Building on a dozen studies correlating friendship and fellowship with health, a new study has found that people with a broad array of social ties are significantly less likely to catch colds than those with sparse social networks. The incidence of infection among people who knew many different kinds of people was nearly half that among those who were relatively isolated, the researchers reported. The lack of diverse social contacts was the strongest of the risk factors for colds that were examined, including smoking, low vitamin C intake, and stress.*

A researcher at Duke University Medical Center found that "heart disease patients with few social ties are six times as likely to die within six months as those with many relatives, friends and acquaintances."

*There you have it—there's power in people!*

Better health is only one of an infinite number of reasons why healthy relationships are so important. The poet John Donne had it right: "No man is an island." Unfortunately, some people try to live like they are—isolated from friends and family, thinking them to be more trouble than they are worth.

Sure, people have faults. But so does the person who's looking for a faultless friend. In fact, his greatest fault is the misconception that perfection in relationships exists. The Hasidic rabbis have a saying that is right on when it comes to relationships: "One who looks for a friend without faults will have none."

Like cells in the human body, we are only healthy—spiritually, emotionally, and physically—when we are doing our part, squeezed right up next to those we can help and who can help us.

According to Dr. James Merritt, a Gallup Poll revealed that by a count of 10-1, people say they prefer a good relationship with the people they love above corporate position or bucks in the bank. And yet the reality is that they invest most of their emotional energy making those dollars and gaining those corporate positions. Why do people say one thing and yet do another?

My friends in counseling professions—ministers, psychologists, psychiatrists, and social workers—say that nearly 100 percent of the counseling they do is because of relationship difficulties: husband-wife, parent-child, teacher-student, employer-employee, neighbor-neighbor, sibling-sibling, and so on. It seems like relationships ought to come naturally, but it is obvious that they don't.

When we come to the end of our lives, it won't be the material things we've accumulated that we'll want surrounding our bed. It will be the people we've loved and those who have loved us in return. Lives of passionate purpose are "others-filled." At the end, if we have created a life we want to live, we will have no regrets about the amount of time we have spent with our loved ones.

# PURPOSE AND MARRIAGE

I willingly and proudly go on record (for the umpteenth time) about the cause for the success I have enjoyed in my career as a speaker and trainer: Had it not been for my wife, Jean, whom I affectionately call "The Redhead," it never would have happened. At the human level, she has been the wind beneath my wings. She has been the one to say, "You can do it," when I needed that affirmation from her.

People who want to be continuously motivated and create a life they want to live need to have the home-court advantage. It's important in basketball, for sure. But the home-court advantage in the NCAA and NBA pales in comparison to the home-court advantage a solid marriage brings.

Since the number one cause of a decline in productivity on the job is marital difficulty at home, and since husbands and wives impact each other so dramatically, it just makes sense to acquire and secure that home-court advantage. When you do you will be more successful on the job, which enables you to provide for your family in a more significant way. You will also experience a reduction in financial stress. Then you can enjoy some of the extra things in life that make it better.

Tom Rath and Donald O. Clifton, PhD, reveal in their book *How Full Is Your Bucket?* that if husbands and wives will follow the 5-1 ratio (five positive observations or comments to their mate for every one that is in any way critical or even dogmatic), the marriage has a magnificent chance of being happy and long-lasting. On the other hand, if there is one negative for every positive comment, divorce is virtually a foregone conclusion. Ten years after they did the original study they discovered they had been 94 percent accurate in diagnosing marriage longevity with the 5-1 ratio rule.

## PURPOSE OF WORK

To the degree it's possible, you should surround yourself with the wisest people you can—people who know things you don't know, who can pull you up to a level higher than where you are today, who can validate or correct your choices as needed. Because we spend so much time in our work settings, the people we interact with become critically important in life, second only to family.

If you are trying to fulfill your true purpose in life, you'll only do it with others' help. Because growth is like the proverbial food chain, everyone is a little further along than someone else. That means you can be a resource, advisor, mentor, or influencer to those younger or less mature than yourself—if you will invest the time and energy in doing so.

The authors of *How Full Is Your Bucket?* reviewed more than 10,000 businesses and more than 30 industries and discovered the following:

- ✤ Individuals who receive regular recognition and praise increase their productivity and stimulate increased engagement among their colleagues. These employees are more likely to stay with the organization, receive higher loyalty and satisfaction scores from customers, and have better safety records and fewer accidents on the job.

- ✤ More than 22 million workers in America are extremely negative or actively disengaged at work, lowering productivity.

- ✤ Sixty-five percent of Americans received no recognition in their workplace the year prior to publication of the book.

❖ Nine out of ten people said they are more productive when they're around positive people.

If you are a business owner, manager, or leader at any level, I hope you saw in those findings some action points to pursue. Part of your purpose in life is to build strong and fruitful relationships with others, and your work setting is a perfect place to start.

People who seek to fulfill their highest purpose in life are those who build and keep winning relationships. There is no better way to do that for a lifetime than to live by the Golden Rule: do unto others as you would have others do unto you. I like to paraphrase that truth this way: you can have everything in life you want if you will just help enough other people get what they want.

Invest in people and you'll create the life you want to live. And the returns will be greater than you can imagine.

"*You can never establish a personal relationship without opening up your own heart.*"

PAUL TOURNIER

# Change Someone's World One Act at a Time

† · † · †

"Love is the only force capable of transforming
an enemy into a friend."

MARTIN LUTHER KING, JR.

*Life is like a relay race in track and field.* The first runner completes his leg and hands the baton off to the second runner, who then gives it to the third, who passes it to the fourth. The smoothness of the handoff has as much to do with the outcome of the race as does the speed of the sprinters.

We do lots of baton passing in life. Parents pass on critical information to their children about faith, love, security, values, and manners. Parents then do a handoff to teachers, coaches, Scout leaders, and others who impart educational, athletic, and service lessons. Then the child, now a young adult, is handed off to college mentors, or perhaps military or vocational trainers, where they learn job skills and additional sets of values and knowledge.

All this time, the way the handoffs and transitions occur is critical. Words of encouragement are like the sticky stuff that is sprayed on the baton to allow each runner to get a firm grip. Sometimes how new information is presented—whether in an encouraging or discouraging fashion—makes all the difference in how it is applied. The world is ultimately changed by the small words and acts that accompany our daily interactions with others.

## YOU, THE PHILANTHROPIST

**What pops into your mind when you hear the word** *philanthropist?* Maybe it's people like Microsoft founder Bill Gates who, along with his wife, has given away $28 billion. Or maybe Intel founder Gordon Moore and his wife, who have given away more than $7 billion. Or Andrew Carnegie who gave away 90 percent of his wealth after he retired (and he was the richest person in the world at that time).

When we see those kinds of numbers in the news we immediately dismiss ourselves from the ranks of significant philanthropists. But not so fast! If you look at the Greek root of our English word *philanthropy* (*philos* = "love"; *anthropos* = "man"), it simply means *"the love of man."*

Thousands of people across our country who have modest bank accounts and incomes are philanthropists in the purest sense of the word. They visit nursing homes and shut-ins to talk, play checkers, listen, and be with the lonely and needy. They read books and magazines to the blind. They deliver food with programs such as Meals on Wheels. They contribute regularly to the Red Cross blood drives. They volunteer as candy stripers in hospitals or as a teacher's aide in inner-city schools. They work in homeless shelters and soup kitchens and they visit inmates in prisons and jails. All of these acts of philanthropy are at the heart of the world's need for loving encouragement. They may not land you on the lists of America's largest donors in terms of money, but you will be at the top of the list among those you touch and serve. Winston Churchill said, "We make a living by what we get; we make a life by what we give."

"But," you say, "I have nothing to give." Wrong. I know of at least one thing you have with you at all times that costs you nothing to acquire or maintain and that has proven to be of tremendous benefit to every person in the world. If I tell you what it is, would you be willing to give it away?

## IT'S YOUR SMILE.

Researchers have identified nineteen different kinds of smiles, each of them capable of communicating a pleasant message that will often be met with a smile in return. A smile is often interpreted as a positive affirmation, an expression of acceptance or pleasure, and, in many cases, love.

When we encounter a person, we look first to his or her face because that's where the signs of life are. If a person has an animated countenance, we feel positive, expecting good things from the encounter. If the person's effect is negative—the brow is furrowed or the face has a scowl—we're put on the defensive. If the effect is flat, or neutral, we're not sure what to expect.

All it takes to set up the potential for a positive encounter with another person is a smile. You obviously have no control over another person's face, but you do have control over yours. By something as simple as wearing a smile you can raise the likelihood of having a positive, fruitful encounter with another person.

Joseph Addison said, "What sunshine is to flowers, smiles are to humanity." They are but trifles, to be sure, but scattered along life's pathway, the good they do is immeasurable.

# YOU, THE YOUTH WORKER

Nothing is more important to the future than the children and young people of today. Everything invested in them now will reap benefits in quantum amounts down the road. And one thing you can give children and young people is an example of what a responsible adult looks like.

Every one of us is a living example to the young people around us. It's not a question of whether we are being watched; it's a question of what the young people are seeing. That which they see, they will reproduce. If you're going to give away your example (and you will), make sure it is one you will be proud to claim years later when you see it reproduced in the life of a young person who watched you.

Ed Shipman and his wife are giving away positive examples of all sorts these days in Granbury, Texas, and it's paying off in spades in the lives of children. The Shipmans founded Happy Hills Farm more than twenty years ago when they took in five foster children. Today, the farm is a widely praised Christian boarding school and working farm for kids with behavioral and academic problems. The faculty and staff (which includes a resident psychologist) oversee 500 beautifully kept acres. Happy Hills refuses all government aid so as to maintain the ability to teach a faith-based curriculum and worldview. Ed personally takes responsibility for raising the school's $3 million annual budget and contributes to that effort by drawing a modest $45,000 salary as the principal of the school.

People who change the world and its future are people who give of themselves out of love (philanthropists), especially to those who will populate the next generation (youth workers). You can be both by giving of those things that you have with you every day: love, your example, a smile, an encouraging word, a philosophy, a worldview, a hope for the future.

"He who reforms himself has done much toward reforming others; and one reason why the world is not reformed is because each would have others make a beginning and never thinks of himself doing it."

THOMAS ADAMS

# Conclusion

## Ready to create a life you want to live?

Then, look to energize the passion, peak performance and purpose in your own life.

Keep the ideas in this book top-of-mind every day for the next thirty days. Change takes time and constant repetition. Feeding your mind new ideas for at least a month is like practicing scales on the piano—you're teaching your mind and body how to do things they've never done before. In time, you'll do them naturally.

Then you will be ready to embrace the quality of life you were meant to have, while accomplishing more than you have ever dreamed possible.

My prayer is that you will discover God's true purpose for your life—a purpose that ignites passion and peak performance. Whether you discover that purpose for the first time, or have that sense of purpose renewed, I believe you can create a life you can't wait to live!

"*Effort matters in everything, love included. Learning to love is purposeful work.*"

MICHAEL LEVINE

# About the Author

Zig Ziglar is an internationally known speaker and the best-selling author of 30 books including the legendary classics See You at the Top and Secrets of Closing the Sale. His works have been translated into more than 40 different languages and dialects. He has been featured on *60 Minutes, The Today Show,* and *20/20*. *Sixty Minutes* says, "He is a legend in the industry — the Bill Gates, Henry Ford and Thomas Edison of enthusiasm."

From humble beginnings in Yazoo City, Mississippi, to being presented with the National Speakers Association's highest award, "The Cavett," Zig Ziglar is recognized by his peers as the quintessential motivational genius of our times. His unique delivery style and powerful messages have earned him many honors. He is considered one of the most versatile authorities on the science of human potential. Having shared the stage with Presidents Ford, Reagan and Bush, Generals Norman Schwarzkopf and Secretary of State Colin Powell, Dr. Norman Vincent Peale, and Paul Harvey, Zig Ziglar is one of the most sought after personal development trainers in the world.

Titans of business, politics and sports consider him to be the single greatest influence in their lives. His client list includes thousands of businesses, Fortune 500 companies, churches, schools, U.S. government agencies and non-profit associations.

Zig Ziglar is known as possibly the greatest encourager who has ever lived. His ability to help people realize their potential is unsurpassed and his belief that, "You can have everything in life you want if you will just help enough other people get what they want," has been the foundation of all he has accomplished.

Zig Ziglar and his wife of 65 years, Jean ("the Redhead"), reside in Plano, Texas, where they attend Prestonwood Baptist Church. He is the father of four children, grandfather of seven and great-grandfather of twelve.

# *What OTHERS are saying...*

We purchased a Simple Truths' gift book for our conference in Lisbon, Spain. We also personalized it with a note on the first page about valuing innovation. I've never had such positive feedback on any gift we've given. People just keep talking about how much they valued the book and how perfectly it tied back to our conference message.

— **Michael R. Marcey,** Efficient Capital Management, LLC.

The small inspirational books by Simple Truths are amazing magic! They spark my spirit and energize my soul.

— **Jeff Hughes,** United Airlines

Mr. Anderson, ever since a friend of mine sent me the 212° movie online, I have become a raving fan of Simple Truths. I love and appreciate the positive messages your products convey and I have found many ways to use them. Thank you for your vision.

— **Patrick Shaughnessy,** AVI Communications, Inc.

If you have enjoyed this book we invite you to check out our entire collection of gift books, with free inspirational movies, at www.simpletruths.com. You'll discover it's a great way to inspire friends and family, or to thank your best customers and employees.

For more information, please visit us at:

# www.simpletruths.com

Or call us toll free... **800-900-3427**